THE POLITICAL MADHOUSE IN
AMERICA AND NEARER HOME

THE
POLITICAL MADHOUSE
IN AMERICA AND
NEARER HOME

A Lecture

by

BERNARD SHAW

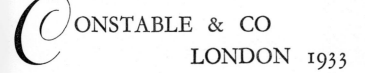

ONSTABLE & CO
LONDON 1933

First Published	.	.	.	.	*August* 1933
Reprinted	.	.	.	.	*August* 1933
Reprinted	.	.	.	.	*August* 1933

PRINTED IN GREAT BRITAIN BY RICHARD CLAY & SONS, LIMITED
BUNGAY, SUFFOLK

AN EXPLANATION

By republishing in England a harangue addressed specifically to Americans in America I lay myself open to an accusation of wantonly holding up my sensitive American friends to British ridicule and contempt, not for their own good, which was my excuse in New York, but solely to gratify our British conceit of moral superiority and the vicious pleasure taken by the meanest of us in the defamation of persons not born in England (mostly in slums).

I am guiltless of any such incivility. It is to rebuke nationalist *Schadenfreude* that I have consented to supply a British counterpart to the edition of my address now circulating in the United States. It would be the silliest hypocrisy to keep up the pleasantry of implying, as I did at the Metropolitan Opera House in New York on the 11th of last April, that the follies and futilities I ascribed to our American cousins are peculiar to their Continent. To please my American audience I made fun of the Hundredpercent American; but the truth is that the Hpc American is a harmless and well-meaning child compared to the Hpc Englishman, Frenchman, German Nazi, or Japanese. The most complete and colossal example of the Hpc American I can recollect was the late William Jennings Bryan, Bi-Metallist, Fundamentalist, and

5

Hot Air Volcano. Shut him off from the rest of the world and measure him by an American scale and it is easy for me or any other critic to make him appear futile as a statesman, absurd as a thinker, and gaseous as an orator. But place him against the sinister figures of the leading British and Continental Hpcs of his generation and it becomes at once apparent that civilization would be much safer in the hands of a batch of Bryans than in theirs. Bryan never said " My country, right or wrong," though he may have sung " My country, 'tis of thee." He never declared that the manifest divine destiny of the entire human race is to be governed by rich young Americans trained in the public schools and universities of the United States. He never came back from a Geneva International Conference and said that of course the United States came first with him, nor sat at a Peace Conference declaring that absolute security for the country in which he happened to be born comes before every other consideration, such absolute security being attainable only by the extermination of everybody except his compatriots, and incidentally of his God (if he believed in one). If he was infatuated about silver he was at least faithful to it, and never won a general election by rallying the nation to its defence immediately before announcing that he was going to save the nation by repudiating it. He did not proclaim the sacredness of ethnographical frontiers, and then, after sacrificing millions of lives to re-establish them, use his victory to establish military frontiers more pregnant with

6

future wars than those he had sworn to redress. In short, Bryan might well pass for an angel of light in contrast with the nationalist patriots of the old world, with their hands against every man and every man's hand against them (except at Peace Conferences where all the said hands slipped surreptitiously into one another's pockets), their reproaches to honest Pacifists for being the friends of every country but their own, and their pride in the alternative of being the enemies of every country but their own. If I have said, as indeed I have, that the Hpc American is an idiot, he may well smile as he wrings my hand cordially for the hundredth time and replies with a smile " At least, dear friend, you do not call me a scoundrel as well."

The main points of my harangue obviously apply to England as urgently as to the United States. As I write, a folly called The World Economic Conference is collapsing in London in an ignominy of failure and futility even greater than that of all the other Conferences by which our Parliament men try to stave off imminent disasters by another bout of talking round them. Obviously a World Economic Conference can succeed only on the assumption by its delegates that under all circumstances two and two make four, always have done so, and always will do so. The delegates in our Museum of Fossils, appropriately selected for their place of meeting, assumed, on the contrary, that the fate of their countries, and finally of the world, is continually being staked on the question whether two and two will make plus fifty million or minus five thousand, as on no other assumption is it worth a financier's while to add two and two together at all. The Conference was bound in the face of Nature to assume that the world must live from hand to mouth on the year's harvest, and can by no sleight of financial or other magic obtain a single grain of wheat from any future year's crop nor a slice from any future year's lamb. But the delegates all accepted as a familiar and unquestionable fact that the next twenty years' harvests are at the immediate disposal of everyone who can pay for them in paper money. The Conference depended on an unshakeable conviction that all real trade is a barter of goods and necessary services, and that where there is no exchange there is robbery. Yet to the delegates trade was only a game at which the player who won the most paper money and lost the most goods was the winner. Nothing could differentiate the Conference from a conspiracy of brigands but a common aspiration to the utmost possible production and cheapening of the necessities and luxuries of a decent life. But the delegates with one voice declared that the only thing that can save the world is a general rise in prices and the destruction by natural calamity or deliberate sabotage of the existing supply of food for lack of which thirty millions of unemployed are perishing by inches. After that it is a mere anti-climax to mention that though sane finance depends on an unsleeping sense that credit is only an opinion, and that men can neither eat it, drink

8

it, nor build houses with it, all the delegates believed that credit is a nourishing and succulent diet, and that as a man with food, drink, and bricks and mortar to the value of a thousand pounds has credit for that sum with his banker, he has in effect a thousand pounds in goods plus a thousand pounds credit, and is therefore " worth " two thousand pounds. " Credit schemes " on this basis are enjoying quite a vogue at present. Straitened nations ask, not for goods, but for credits.

I have not time to complete the analysis of the dust storm of delusions which constituted the mental equipment of the delegates. The Russian delegate was the only one who proceeded on mentionable assumptions; and he confessed that his reason was giving way under the strain of having to argue with a World Conference of incurable lunatics. He was saved by his sense of humor; but his sense of humor could not save the world situation. The lunatics have gone home to their respective national asylums; but they are still in charge there; and if our affairs are not taken out of their hands we shall go to smash. For their greatest lunacy of all is that not one of them can see the smallest reason why any human being should be allowed to live unless in addition to supporting himself he can produce a privately appropriable profit for a shareholder or a rent for a landlord. Why, they argue, should anyone organize the work of property-less men merely to produce their own food? Rather let them perish, or, if they shew signs of muttering " Thou shalt starve ere I starve," let the tax collector collect some crumbs for them from the owners' tables. At such a point youths of spirit become car bandits and racketeers and kidnappers. What else do our crazy conference-mongers expect? It is easy to say " If you cannot produce a profit get off the earth : you have no right to live." Proletarians are so blind to this point of view that in the final issue they reply " Que messieurs les assassins commencent."

I therefore conciliate my American friends by inviting my English ones to apply everything I say of the Americans in this book to themselves with the assurance that they deserve it no less, and that their day of judgment may be no further off, if so far.

G. B. S.

Ayot St. Lawrence,
  16th July, 1933.

$\mathcal{M}$R. CHAIRMAN, LADIES AND GENTLEMEN: Finding myself in an opera house with such a magnificent and responsive audience, I feel an irresistible temptation to sing. But I am afraid my unfortunate age precludes any performance of that kind.

I drag in the subject of my age because it has something to do with what I am going to say to-night. I am, of course, perfectly aware of how old men try to foist on the public the decay of their intellects and all the rest of their senile shortcomings as valuable qualities, the possession of which gives them special authority.

Dont you believe them, ladies and gentle-men. It does not give them any authority except on one subject. The sole advantage my age gives me over the majority of my audience is that I have actually seen about three generations of human beings.

11

I was born seventy-seven years ago into a world of what seemed to me to be very grown-up and middle-aged and old people; and in the course of time I had to grow up myself. I have carried infants in my arms, and seen those infants enlarge themselves and have infants of their own and become elderly or middle aged, and finally die. And therefore I can look back and speak with first-hand experience of generations of people whom you never met.

I can remember the sort of person an American was, say, in the year 1861. I was already old enough to read the newspapers and to see in them every day the heading, THE CIVIL WAR IN AMERICA.

The American of that day was quite unlike the American of to-day, thank Heaven! I dare say all of you young people must be a little puzzled by a curious figure that still turns up from time to time in your political caricatures—I mean the figure of Uncle Jonathan. I have been in the United States now for some days; but I have not yet seen a single individual who bears the very remotest resemblance to Uncle Jonathan.

Uncle Jonathan is dead. He is gone: he has vanished. But when I was a boy Uncle

12

Jonathan really did exist. The Americans of those days were not really Americans at all. They were emigrants ; they were provincials ; they were people bringing to America the habits of an old country and an old civilization : all the bad habits as well as the good ones. They were setting up for themselves as a first-hand nation in second-hand clothes with a very uneasy self-consciousness which made them ridiculously sensitive to any remarks made by foreigners about them.

Even to this day it is easier than it ought to be for me to get a rise out of an American by telling him something about himself which is equally true about every human being on the face of the globe. He at once resents this as a disparagement and an assertion on my part that people in other parts of the globe are not like that, and are loftily superior to such weaknesses.

This exiled British provincial who was not a genuine American, but an immigrant from another country, this man who had nothing distinctively American about him except the name of Yankee, this villager who had the sort of education a Christian missionary gives to a Negro child, with the corresponding primitive culture : this was the bygone American of seventy-five years ago.

He went on for a long time trying to do the things that Europe was doing, and doing them very badly, I may remark, though generally very expensively. But at last there emerged a sort of American amazingly unlike Uncle Jonathan, or any other sort of man on earth. To begin with, he was considerably fleshier ; but beyond that he was something which it is very hard to describe.

He was a colossal person : he was an extremely dignified person. When you met him, you felt that here was a man of commanding importance : a man who had something in him. But you never could get that something out of him. He was a tremendous talker, a rhetorician of magnificent periods and splendid perorations, an orator who shouted at meetings and pontificated at dinner tables at great length. But he never said anything. It was pure oratory for oratory's sake : a branch of Art for Art's sake. You cheered him enthusiastically, and felt that now something was going to happen at last. It never did.

He was a bombinating sort of man, if I may coin the expression. He was monumental; but he was so void of anything new or different that we in Europe staggered when we contemplated his immensity and its utter insignificance. We said, what is the secret of this tremendous man, who talks so splendidly and has nothing to say? This man whose mind, although it is evidently an intensely live mind, might just as well be an intense absence of mind, because he doesnt seem to know anything of any particular consequence. He is always in a state of vociferous excitement about entirely trivial things. He quotes the poets thunderously to give point to piffle.

I am very much tempted to mention one famous American, now deceased, who was true to this type; but I need not, because all of you will be able—those of you, at any rate, who are getting on a little in life—to put a name to him. You will say " Oh yes : he means So-and-So, Senator So-and-So or Congressman So-and-So," or some as yet unelected monument.

Now, what was wrong with this sort of man was that he had no intellectual bearings. He had no general modern theory of society. He had no American theory of American society. If I may borrow an expression from my friend Professor Archibald Henderson, who is a mathematician, he had no frame of reference. He had no scientific postulates of any kind. He was in the air ; consequently you got nothing out of him but wind— though it is true you got a terrific quantity of that.

Such was—and is—the human phenomenon who emerged from the old Uncle Jonathans, and astonished the world as the Hundred-percent American. He was unique. I have travelled a good deal ; but I never saw in any other country anybody like the Hundred-percent American.

He presented himself to Europe as a dog-matic politician ; and it was precisely as a dogmatic politician that he was a complete failure. What was wrong with him was that he had no political constitution to which he could refer his dogmas.

Now if you had told him that, he would have come as near fainting as is possible to a monument. He would have said " What ! no political constitution ? No such thing as a constitution in America ! Are you mad ? America has got *the* constitution *par excellence*. America is always talking about its Constitution."

To which an Englishman, if he were tact-less, would say "America is always talking about its Constitution; but as it is also always amending its Constitution, it looks as if that Constitution were not quite so perfect as you seem to suppose."

When you came to examine the American Constitution, you found that it was not really a Constitution but only a Charter of Anar-chism. It was not an instrument of govern-ment: it was a guarantee to the whole American nation that it never should be governed at all. And that is exactly what the Americans want.

The ordinary man—we have to face it: it is every bit as true of the ordinary English-man as of the ordinary American—is an Anarchist. He wants to do as he likes. He may want his neighbor to be governed, but he himself doesnt want to be governed. He is mortally afraid of government officials and policemen. He loathes tax collectors. He shrinks from giving anybody any official power whatever. This Anarchism has been at work in the world since the beginnings of civilization; and its supreme achievement up to date is the American Constitution.

It is a formidable instrument, explicit in

black and white. In England we have the British Constitution; but nobody knows what it is: it is not written down anywhere; and you can no more amend it than you can amend the east wind. But in the United States you have a real tangible readable document. I can nail you down to every one of its sentences.

. And what does it amount to? A great protest against the tyranny of law and order. A final manifesto from the centuries of revolutionary Anarchism in which the struggle went on against government as such, against government by feudal barons, by autocratic Kings, by the Pope and his cardinals, by the parliaments which have gradually ousted all these authorities, each of them in turn being used to disable the others in the glorified cause of what people called Liberty, until, having destroyed the king, the barons, the Church, and finally all effective parliamentary governing power, you found yourselves hopelessly under the thumbs of your private racketeers, from the humble gunman to the great financial magnate, each playing for his own hand without status, without national authority or responsibility, without legal restraint and without any sense of public government. You had perfected a Constitution of negatives to defend liberty, liberty, liberty—life, liberty, and the pursuit of happiness—against the only checks on anarchy that could secure them, and fortified it by a Supreme Court which dealt out nothing but prohibitions, and a political party machinery of legislatures and senates, which was so wonderfully devised that when you sent in one body of men to govern the country, you sent in another body of men along with them to prevent their doing it. In your dread of dictators you established a state of society in which every ward boss is a dictator, every financier a dictator, every private employer a dictator, all with the livelihood of the workers at their mercy, and no public responsibility.

And to symbolize this state of things, this defeat of all government, you have set up in New York Harbour a monstrous idol which you call Liberty. The only thing that remains to complete that monument is to put on its pedestal the inscription written by Dante on the gate of Hell " All hope abandon, ye who enter here."

Still, I must not reproach you; for you might remind me that you took your Anarchism straight from England, parliament, party system, second chamber and all, and that we are just as incapable as you of doing anything as a nation except talk, talk, talk endlessly. But I do reproach you for a special American propaganda of Anarchism which is having most serious effects throughout the world. Formerly you were not able to affect public morals and public feeling much on the other side of the Atlantic. But now you have an instrument called the cinematograph and a centre called Hollywood, which has brought public and private morals under your influence everywhere.

An eminent American, whom I will not name, has sent me a letter which I received yesterday morning. It says "Do not judge the United States by its two plague spots: Hollywood and New York."

I was not surprised. Hollywood is the most immoral place in the world. But you do not realize this, because the moment I use the word "immoral," every American begins to think of ladies' underclothing. So please do not suppose that I am talking of that very necessary thing, sex appeal, the use of which in the theatre and in the cinema is most desirable, provided it be well done, and the sex appeal made really educational, as it can be.

No : the doctrine with which Hollywood is corrupting the world is the doctrine of Anarchism. Hollywood keeps before its child audiences a string of glorified young heroes, everyone of whom is an unhesitating and violent Anarchist. His one answer to everything that annoys him or disparages his country or his parents or his young lady or his personal code of manly conduct, is to give the offender a " sock " in the jaw.

Why do you not prosecute the film corporations for inciting all our youths to breaches of the peace ? Why do you applaud these screen heroes who, when they are not kissing the heroine, are socking jaws ? It is a criminal offence to sock a citizen in the jaw. When shall we see a film issuing from Hollywood in which the hero acts like a civilized man, and, instead of socking somebody in the jaw, calls a policeman ?

I notice that you receive this coldly. You think perhaps that the policeman would bore you. He could never bore you, at his very worst, ladies and gentlemen, as those eternal socks in the jaw bore me, and bore every civilized person. Try to get rid of them.

Above all, try to get rid of the ignorant Anarchism that is at the back of them—that notion that moral law is something that every man may take into his own hands as judge and jury in his own case, and execute with his own fist.

Besides, my observation leads me to believe that it is not the virtuous people who are good at socking jaws. The Providence which is on the side of the big battalions is also apt to favor the quickest and hardest hitters.

But now let us get back to the American Constitution. People are beginning to find out that Constitution. The Hundredpercent American is being succeeded by a more highly developed American. He is more muscular and less adipose than the Hundred-percent American. He has the same imposing presence, the same eloquence, the same vitality, the same dignity, the same enthusiasm. But his dignity is not pompous ; and his enthusiasm is attached to definite measures and not to selections from the poetry and rhetoric of the day before yesterday.

I hope Mr. Franklin Roosevelt is a sample of that new American. I think my friend Mr. William Randolph Hearst anticipated him years ago. At all events I mention these two gentlemen not only because they illustrate what I mean, but because the main symptom of the change is that they are both very violently against the Constitution. President Roosevelt is appealing to you at the present time to get rid of your confounded Constitution, and give him power to govern the country. He hopes that if you do he will be able to govern it. But he knows he must fail as long as Congress is there to prevent him.

You have tried constitutional presidents before, ladies and gentlemen. You have tried again and again. You tried Mr. Hoover. Mr. Hoover had shewn himself a capable and practical man in certain transactions, connected with feeding people during the war. On that ground you elected him. You wanted a practical man. You were in a practical mood.

You found him of no use whatever as President. He ceased to be a practical man. Congress would not let him be a practical man. The Constitution was not practical. Everything ended in talk, talk, talk. Then, during his term of office, you had a bad slump. Your political, social and industrial system registered signs of a first-rate earthquake somewhere ; and when the Constitution made it impossible for Mr. Hoover to save you, you revenged yourself on him by throwing him out. I suppose I must not say you kicked him out, but you certainly sent him to the foot of the poll with extraordinary violence. And then you turned to Mr. Roosevelt. Why ?

Because, as the practical mood in which you elected Mr. Hoover was a disappointment, you reacted into a sentimental mood. Just then Mr. Roosevelt, by a happy chance, got photographed with a baby. The baby was a success : Mr. Roosevelt went to the White House in its arms. I dont know whether the baby is still there ; but I know that you hope a great deal from Mr. Franklin Roosevelt. Well, you will get nothing from him if he has to act constitutionally through the usual routine of Congress. His four years will inevitably end in as great a disappointment as Mr. Hoover's.

In the meantime, Mr. Hoover has gone back into practical business life where things are meant to be done, and has been discovered again to be perfectly successful as a practical man.

The body I am speaking for here to-night—by the way, it is not responsible for everything I say—is the Academy of Political Science. What is its first and most pressing job ? Evidently to smash the American Constitution. To get rid of it at all hazards.

That seems easy enough, because your Constitution has for a long time been getting rid of itself bit by bit through endless amendments. But it cannot be wholly discarded until this Academy achieves the far more difficult feat of supplying a new Constitution. That is what it is for. It has no other purpose. And will you kindly tell all your friends that there is such a thing as political science, because most of them dont know it. They know that there is such a thing as electioneering ; and perhaps they occasionally take part in one of those scandalous and disgusting spectacles that are called election meetings, at which sane and sober men yell senselessly until any dispassionate stranger looking at them would believe that he was in a lunatic asylum for exceptionally dreadful cases of mental derangement. I hope you all look forward to the time when such disgraces will become impossible in this and every other country. I am speaking now from guilty experience. I have stood on election

platforms ; I have made speeches ; I have
had audiences rising with enthusiasm at the
conclusion of my addresses and singing " For
He's a Jolly Good Fellow ! " You will not
do that at the conclusion of my present
speech, because you dont know the tune in
this country. You need not regret it ; for
my candidates were mostly defeated. But
defeated or not I have never spoken nor
listened at an election meeting without being
ashamed of the whole sham democratic routine. The older I grow the more I feel such
exhibitions to be, as part of the serious
business of the government of a nation,
entirely intolerable and disgraceful to human
nature and civic decency.

I am listening to the curious dead silence
which shews that you all agree with me,
but that you are rather doubtful (*applause*)—
Ah ! There it comes !

If you feel that way there may be some
hope for the Academy of Political Science
after all. But I must warn you that it is
very doubtful whether Man is enough of a
political animal to produce a good, sensible,
serious and efficient political constitution. It
is an open question, I quite admit. So far,
all the evidence is against it.

26

Within my lifetime our knowledge of history has been greatly extended. We used to be taught that antiquity meant the Roman Empire, which had absorbed the Greek city States with the pyramids of Egypt looking on, and with Jerusalem and a sketchy Babylonian collection of idolators in the hinterland. The one belief that we got out of it all was that modern civilization was an immense improvement on those barbarous times, and that all white people had been steadily progressing, getting less and less superstitious, less and less savage, more and more enlightened, until the pinnacle had been reached, represented by ourselves.

We are now beginning to have serious doubts whether we ourselves are in any way remarkable or unprecedented as specimens of political enlightenment ; for our new knowledge of history tells us that our picture of the past was false. Thanks largely to the researches of Professor Flinders Petrie, we know of five or six ancient civilizations which were just like our own civilization, having progressed in the same way, to the same artistic climaxes, the same capitalistic climaxes, the same democratic and feminist climaxes as we ; and they all perished. They reached a certain point and then collapsed, because they had no internal stability. When they grew into huge populations crowded into big cities without equality of class or income the internal strains set up by the inequalities shattered them, and civilization sank back again into primitive life for the survivors.

That puts us in a very different mental attitude from our fathers and grandfathers, because what we are up against now is the fact that we too have reached the edge of the precipice over which these civilizations fell and were dashed to pieces. There is no mistaking the situation : the symptoms are the same ; the difficulties are the same ; and the possibilities of rapid destruction are much greater. Are we going to bridge the gulf or fall helplessly into it ? Can we, if I may change the metaphor, steer our ship round the headlands on which all the ancient navigators were wrecked ?

I dont know whether we are or not, ladies and gentlemen. I have very often expressed an opinion that it does not very much matter whether we do or not, because if we fail, some other sort of creature will appear on the earth to carry on the work that has beaten us. You see, I do not, like the Fundamentalists, believe that creation stopped six thousand years ago after a week of hard work. Creation is going on all the time. I believe that if mankind proves, for the fifth or sixth time to our present knowledge, that it is a hopeless political failure, then the same power that created us will create a race capable of getting round the headlands and making America a political success. And if that supermanly race be provided with a gun, I am afraid we shall be the first victims of its superior intelligence and superior power.

But we must not and indeed cannot proceed on the assumption that we are failures. We may have suspicions of our own shortcomings; but we are bound to try to get round these headlands. The Academy of Political Science is organized to try to find out how to do it. Why have we not done it already? What is wrong with us? And assuming that we find out what is wrong with us, have we the strength of character to remedy it?

This brings me back to the Hundredpercent American. To some extent he is a pet of mine. I have always rather liked him, because he has some promising qualities. For instance, he has enormous hospitality. I used to feel personally complimented by the amazing warm-hearted hospitality showered on me by Americans. But its scope is so boundless that I now perceive that it lies in the nature of the host rather than in the quality of the guest. Even women are hospitable in America. An American woman seems to have no other object in life than to fill her house with other people, even when she does the cooking herself. When I realized it, I began to say to myself, " This is not a recognition of my own particular merits. Nor is it quite a mania. There is something bigger behind it. An enormous social instinct must be seeking satisfaction through it."

Then I considered your rage for publicity. An American has no sense of privacy. He does not know what it means. There is no such thing in the country. The English have it very strongly. An Englishman very often fails in business where an American would succeed, because the Englishman, when he opens a shop, or hotel, or any other place of public resort, instead of welcoming a customer, cannot help treating him as an unwarrantable intruder who has come into his shop without a proper introduction. The American does not feel like that. He has public instinct, social feeling. You see it not only in his hospitality, but in his love of lectures and public meetings, his eagerness to hear anybody who will talk and shake hands with him afterwards. You, ladies and gentlemen, have just parted with sums of money that are quite considerable during the present crisis. What to do? To hear me talk. You did not know what I was going to say. You guessed that I should not hand you the usual visitor's bouquets. But you love talk because there is something public about it. There is promise of public action in it. And I, having watched this through my long life, have begun to see that it is also a force which may turn into volcanic political genius if it gets mixed with brains and knowledge.

If only it can get a positive Constitution, if it can find sound intellectual bearings, if it can devise (again I quote the mathematicians) a frame of reference within which its brains can work, possibly America may save human society yet by solving the great political problems which have baffled and destroyed all previous attempts at permanent civilization. I have hopes, because America has got this irrepressible social instinct, this wonderful surging thing inside itself, that you do not find in the same reckless profusion elsewhere. Will that carry you through? Has America the entrails to do the job? If I were in England I should use a shorter word; but in America I am told I must be careful.

You know, if you study American history— not the old history books; for almost all American histories, until very lately, were mere dustbins of the most mendacious vulgar journalism—but the real history of America, you will be ashamed of it because the real history of all mankind is shameful. But there is hope in bits of it. I wonder how many of you have ever studied the history of the Latter Day Saints: one of the most extraordinary episodes in the white settlement of the world. You should do so; for it shews Americans doing something for reasons which would astonish me very much if I saw the same thing being done for the same reasons in England.

There was a time when the Mormons were so few in number that they were in very great danger of being killed by their pious neighbors because their views were unpopular. But they were themselves a very pious people. They were brought up with the strictest old-fashioned ideas with regard to the relations of the sexes and the sanctity of marriage: marriage, of course, being the established monogamous marriage of the Christian west.

Well, their leader went to these pious men and women and said to them "I want you to take to polygamy. I want all you men to have as many wives as you can possibly afford instead of one wife."

Think what a terrific thing that was to say to such people! I do not know any more moving passage in literature than that in which Brigham Young describes how, after receiving this appalling order, he met a funeral on his way home and found himself committing the mortal sin of envying the dead. And yet Brigham Young lived to have a very large number of wives according to our ideas—thirty something, I think it was—and to become immortal in history as an American Moses by leading his people through the wilderness into an unpromised land where they founded a great city on polygamy.

Now nothing can be more idle, nothing more frivolous, than to imagine that this polygamy had anything to do with personal licentiousness. If Joseph Smith had proposed to the Latter Day Saints that they should live licentious lives, they would have rushed on him and probably anticipated the pious neighbors who presently shot him. The significant point in the case was that the reason he gave them was a purely political reason. He said " Unless we multiply our numbers, we are lost ; and we can multiply our numbers rapidly only by polygamy. And, therefore, whatever our prejudices, whatever our feelings may be, if we are to save the Church of the Latter Day Saints from annihilation by the superior numbers of its enemies in this State, we must take to polygamy."

And they did it. That was the wonderful American thing. A body of Americans were capable of changing their lives and discarding their most deeply rooted ideas for a purely political reason ! That makes some of you laugh. I am very glad. Whenever in the search for truth I hit the nail exactly on the head, there is always a laugh at first ; but nothing that I shall say to-night is more significant than that illustration of American capacity for political action, in view of the necessity to the United States of a new Constitution. I really do entertain a hope—I think I am the only person in the world who entertains it so far—perhaps after my preaching to-night some of you may consider it—that you Americans, in spite of your follies in the past, in spite of your obsolete Uncle Jonathan, in spite of your ridiculous Hundredpercent American, may yet take the lead in political thought and action, and help to save the soul of the world.

I admit that your existing situation is not a very promising one. Your proletariat is unemployed. That means the breakdown of your capitalist system, because, as any political scientist will tell you, the whole justification of the system of privately appropriated capital and land on which you have been working, is its guarantee, elaborately reasoned out on paper by the capitalist economists, that although one result of it must be the creation of a small but enormously rich propertied class which is also an idle class, living at the expense of the propertyless masses who are getting only a bare living, nevertheless that bare living is always secured for them. There must always be employment available ; and they will always be able to obtain a subsistence wage for their labor.

When that promise is broken (and never for one moment has it been kept right up to the hilt), when your unemployed are not only the old negligible five per cent. of this trade, eight per cent. of that trade, two per cent. of the other trade, but millions of unemployed, then the capitalist system has broken down ; and your most pressing job is to find a better one.

Passing from your starving proletariat, what about your farmers ? Your farmers are bankrupt ; and they are in armed revolt. Even the newspapers tell you this if you read them carefully, although in all civilized countries at present newspapers exist for the purpose of concealing the truth from the public in such matters.

What about your employers ? When I was a young man, the employer in America was master of the industrial situation. He employed the proletariat on his own account and for his own profit. He employed the land of the landlord and paid him a rent for it. He employed the capital of the capitalists and paid them interest for it. What remained was his own. Thus he had the whole business of the country in his hands, and was undisputed cock of the walk in all industrial republics. And any man who could read and write and cipher, and had a reasonable share of business ability, could start as an employer with a little capital either saved by himself or borrowed from his family or his friends.

All that is gone. The ordinary employer of to-day belongs to the proletariat. He is an employed manager, living on a salary with perhaps a percentage to encourage him to work for others as hard as he formerly did for himself. Scientific discovery has revealed new methods of producing wealth which require enormous plants costing prodigious amounts of capital. The old-fashioned employer was a very considerable person when he could command a capital of five thousand dollars. To-day the dollars needed to start big enterprises are counted in hundreds of millions ; and the ordinary employer is utterly unable to find such sums or to prevent the big enterprises swallowing up his little ones. He has, therefore, fallen helplessly into the power of a class of men whose business it is to find millions, the financiers. They are the present masters of the situation.

37

Your country is run by them. Just now they are running it into the ditch; but you still let them run it.

To impress on you how extraordinarily dangerous is the condition of a country which lets itself be governed by private financiers, may I shew you the sort of person a private financier is ? He is the very contrary of a statesman. The financier is always thinking about what a single individual with money can do at a favorable moment if it pleases him. But the statesman has to consider what millions of individuals, with or without money, can be forced by law to do every day whether they like it or not. That is how the financier's mind forms fixed habits which make him incapable of the point of view of the statesman, who has to remember at every legislative step " Here is something that everybody, rich or poor, will have to do simultaneously if I make this law."

Now, one of the things that somebody can always do, and that everybody can never do is this. Suppose you have a little pension —for simplicity I will put it at five dollars a year—and you say " This pension of five dollars is not much : I would rather have a big spree and be done with it; or I would

38

like to start a little business with it." Accordingly you go to the ordinary rank-and-file financier called a stockbroker, and say " Look here. I have a settled income of five dollars a year ; but I want to raise a hundred dollars. Could you get me a hundred dollars for my five dollars a year ? " The stockbroker will reply " Certainly. It is perfectly easy. I shall just find somebody who has a hundred dollars more than he need spend, and would like to exchange it for an addition of five dollars a year to his permanent income. Nothing simpler. It is done every day."

Wall Street and the Stock Exchanges and the Bourses are only large markets in which people exchange incomes for ready money just in this way. One man's spare money buys him an addition to his income ; and another man's income buys him a lump sum of ready money. The vast majority who have neither independent incomes to sell nor ready money to spare are not concerned nor considered at all.

The professional financier who is doing this kind of business all the time—whose mind and soul are steeped in Wall Street and the Stock Exchanges, gets a fixed habit of multiplying all the resources of the country on paper by twenty. You see the process. To him every man who has five dollars a year is worth a hundred dollars. He is quite certain of that, because he knows that at any moment he can go into the money market and obtain a hundred dollars in exchange for an income of five dollars. He knows also that twenty times five make a hundred. And there you are !

What happens when you make your financiers statesmen ? Their first duty is to find out how much taxation you can bear. For that they must find out how much wealth there is in your hands to tax. They order a clerk to calculate the entire wealth of the United States. The clerk immediately finds out from the income tax returns what is the total income of the country, multiplies it by twenty, and hands in the product as the wealth available for immediate taxation in the United States. Not having a statesman's mind he forgets that if all the people with incomes are driven by law to sell them simultaneously, the Stock Exchange will become a market in which there are all sellers and no buyers, and the value of their securities will be just exactly zero.

That is to say, financiers live in a world of

illusion. They count on something which they call the capital of the country which has no existence. Every five dollars they count as a hundred dollars ; and that means that every financier, every banker, every stockbroker, is 95 per cent. a lunatic. And it is in the hands of these lunatics that you leave the fate of your country !

You also give them a certain hidden power, greater than any public political power, which exists in all large and rich commercial communities. That power is the power latent in banking. How does it arise ? Very simply. In a village people can keep their spare money, if they have any, in an old stocking, or bury it in the back garden ; but in towns men of business have to handle large sums which they want to have kept safely for them and paid out to their order as and when they need it. They began by leaving their money with the goldsmiths, who were quite willing to keep it for them and let them have it when they had payments to make. You see, the goldsmiths discovered, not by the exercise of any skill on their part, but simply by experiencing what happened, that if they had a large number of people leaving money with them and never drawing it all out—

keeping a balance as we call it—they would
have a lot of other people's money to play
with all the time. Take my own case. I
am only a private professional man; but it
is necessary for the conduct of my business
and household that I always keep at my
bank about £1,000 at call. When the sum
falls below that I replenish it. The consequence is that my banker is in a permanent
condition of having £1,000 of mine; and
if you add to my poor professional man's
little £1,000 the huge balances needed by
the big industrial corporations, and the multi-
tude of modest margins from the smaller fry,
you will see how when the goldsmiths became
bankers they found that an astonishing pro-
portion of the money lodged with them
remained permanently in their hands, enabling
them to enter on the most lucrative of all
businesses : the business of money-lending
with other people's money.

They ran only one risk, and that was that
if all their customers were seized with panic
and made a simultaneous rush to draw out
their money, the money would not be there ;
and the bank would break, just as the Bank
of England broke the other day because
there was a run on gold. But this occurs so

seldom that the risk is negligible; and as the Bank of England is still able to pay twelve or thirteen shillings in the pound, its bankruptcy is politely called going off the gold standard.

But now you see that this natural discovery made by the goldsmiths and exploited by them as bankers, sets up automatically in large civilizations like yours a money power so irresistible that it becomes a political and industrial power, not to say a religious power, of the most formidable magnitude. Any nation that leaves this power in the hands of irresponsible private men to use simply for their own enrichment, is either politically ignorant or politically mad to the utmost possible degree.

You applaud; but this is exactly what you are doing. The smallest smattering of political science will tell you that the first thing you must do to get out of your present mess is to nationalize your banks. Well, why not nationalize them instead of merely applauding me?

All the political advice given by financiers since the War, has, as you know, been wrong advice. There has been only one great man in the banking world, Montagu Norman of the Bank of England ; and he has said the final banker's word about the money problem. That word is " I dont understand it." No wonder ; for there is no problem to understand. Money is just what it always was and always will be.

I must mention one or two other delusions from which financiers suffer. If you read the money articles in the papers, you will notice that the prosperity of a country is always measured at present by the money it receives for its exports. " A favorable balance of trade " is what the financiers clamor for ; and by a favorable balance of trade they mean an excess of exports over imports. Now this seems reasonable enough to people who think in terms of money. To people who think in terms of goods it is raving nonsense. Foreign trade is nothing but barter conducted with money ; and to maintain that in barter the more you give and the less you get in exchange the more prosperous you are, is to qualify yourself for the asylum. Yet in America and England it qualifies you for the Cabinet. A financier cannot think in terms of bread and butter or bricks and mortar : he thinks in figures. He has never been inside a factory or down a mine or on

44

a farm. Sending goods out of the country means to him nothing but attracting money into it. His ideal is a country which exports everything it produces, and gets nothing in return but title deeds to gold, of which you in America have too much already.

This craze for getting money into the country makes the financier very keen on foreign investments. To begin with, he makes a good deal of money by floating foreign loans ; and the first effect of the foreign loan is to stimulate exports. But the ultimate effect is to annihilate exports by producing a state of things in which the nation lives on an income which comes from abroad as interest on the foreign loan, and exports nothing in return. The financier is caught in his own trap ; and you are caught with him. He wants more exports, more exports, and still more exports. To stimulate them he organizes foreign investments which mean more imports, more imports, and still more imports. He is working at the same time for a policy of producing and exporting everything, and for a policy of importing everything and producing nothing.

The result of these two contrary impulses struggling in his brain is, that you revere him as an omniscient master of finance when he has reduced himself to nothing but a neurotic gambler with an insoluble complex. If it were not that his left hand is continually undoing the work of his right he would have ruined you long ago.

What are the risks of this policy of stimulating exports, and judging your prosperity solely by their excess over imports ? They are quite incompatible with international peace and domestic prosperity. Foreign competition is always trying to take away the markets for your exports. That leads to war in the long run. If you lose your markets, you have to go after fresh markets ; and that leads to imperial invasion and conquest abroad. Foreign trade also brings your own workers into competition with the poorest workers on earth. The coolie who works for two cents a day sets the standard of life for your own proletariat ; and that leads to strikes, riots, and civil war.

So much for the risks of the export policy. Now what about the imports ? Suppose by the advice of your financial experts you send all your capital out of the United States to the places where labor is cheapest, and settle down to live on the interest from foreign

46

investments, ceasing to produce industrial profits, or to produce even your own food ! Well, that is a golden prospect, is it not ? All America would be like Atlantic City. The whole coast would become a magnificent Miami Beach. You would have music, dancing, night clubs ; you would have beautifully dressed girls ; you would live in hotels with jazz bands and cabarets at every meal when you were not cruising round the world in perpetual sunshine in luxury liners. Quite a paradise, wouldnt it be ? A great many people appear to think so. It would not suit me personally ; but I am notoriously eccentric.

Well, what are the risks, if any, of that ? They are rather serious. For instance, repudiation by the other countries of the interest on which you are living ! You may have repudiation with revolution as in Russia. You may have repudiation without revolution as in France, which has calmly repudiated 80 per cent. of her War loan. And what about the politer form of repudiation known as foreign income tax ? Every foreign country has an unlimited power of taxing at the source all the dividends payable out of its industries. It can levy a tax of a hundred cents on every dollar. You used to tax my

Liberty Loan unblushingly; and you still tax my hard earned royalties on the ground that it is your actors and printers who do the hard earning. There is even a risk of war to wipe the slate. The countries on which you are depending may find it cheaper to fight you and get rid of the burden, with a chance of being able to live on you instead of allowing you to live on them. And then where are you? You have become a wonderful night clubby sort of nation; but there is nothing so helpless as a raided night club.

Yet your financiers are always driving you in this direction, just as by another road they are driving you in the opposite direction. Either way they are tempting you to run the most terrible risks, risks which will eventually destroy you if you persist. But do not blame the financiers. They are quite honest and patriotic. They do it in their own business, and it works; and they think if it is done in everybody's business it must work. That is why you must breed statesmen who will supersede the financier and put him back in his proper private place.

Let me take a capital instance. We had a war in Europe. You lent Europe about five milliards of dollars, on England's security.

48

What value did you get for that ? You got the destruction of three European empires, and the substitution of American republicanism for monarchical rule as the typical national rule in Europe. Most European Kings are now exiles and outcasts. The rest are what you call constitutional monarchs, which means that they are not monarchs at all, and consequently have a fairly pleasant and popular time of it. I suggest that this was pretty fair value for your money. But you got something more remarkable than that, that will be yet more important in the future : you achieved the salvation of Russia. I gather from your applause that at last I have met some Americans who know that they saved Russia.

Russia, when the tsardom fell, tried your form of government. It set up what it calls a bourgeois republic. The country was in the most desperate need of reconstruction ; but the bourgeois republic could do nothing but talk, just like Congress. It collapsed helplessly when the Bolsheviks took the situation in hand and imposed a real positive government on the distracted and starving country. That government had a terrible job to face. There was Russia with her popu-

D   49

lation of one hundred and sixty million ignorant and half savage peasants, knowing nothing about modern industrial development, not knowing how to handle machinery. There had been a little industrialism before the war; but it was all in the hands of Englishmen, of Belgians, of Italians, and of Germans. Yet when the new Russian rulers, having to rescue this enormous population from famine, savagery, ignorance, dirt and slavery, could do so only by establishing the machinery of modern industry in Russia at all costs, and did not know how to do it, did they turn for instruction to their old exploiters, the English, the Belgians, the Italians, and the Germans? No. By some sort of inspiration, they turned to America; and America saved them. They were guided by the advice and instruction of your American efficiency engineers. The American efficiency engineers did not flatter them. They came and looked, and said " Your condition is appalling: you are making a disastrous mess of your attempts at modern machine industry. It seems utterly impossible that you should ever get out of that mess. We can tell you what to do; but whether your untrained peasants can do it is another matter." And they told them. I know the American who took to Moscow the very remarkable report in which the information was given. That gentleman passed through London on his way, and submitted the report to some English experts. The English experts made some valuable suggestions; but they said " Do you suppose the Russians will tolerate such an exposure of their inefficiency as this ? Go and hand in your report, and they will hand you back across the frontier the next day. They will suppress that report; and nobody will ever hear of it again."

Well, your fellow countrymen, representing an able American firm, said " That will not matter to us. The Russians have paid for a report; we shall give it to them; and they can do what they like with it. They can suppress it as an English or American government would; but at any rate they will get what they paid for and get it good."

The English experts were mistaken. Within forty-eight hours of the handing in of the report in Moscow, the Russians had ten thousand printed copies of it in circulation; and their loud speakers all over the country were shouting out the lessons of the report and telling the Russian workmen that all the waste and breakages and blundering must stop, and that they must learn how to operate and care for their own machines. American workmen were invited to Russia to teach factory work, and American managers to teach factory management ; and now, as you know, Russia has pulled through, even though her American teachers said that it was hardly conceivable that she could under the circumstances. You see, the Russian producers were free from the frightful friction of competition that wastes so much in our countries, where every manager is fighting for profit against every other manager, and every factory divided against itself by class conflict. The Russians pulled through because they all pulled together ; and the result is that they are now one of the biggest industrial powers in the world, thanks to America.

Some of you may say candidly " This is very gratifying in a way ; but did we quite intend to do it ? " Well, perhaps not ; but may not the blind political instinct which I have given you credit for have carried you on in spite of yourselves to do the right thing ? At all events you helped to establish Communism in Russia ; and it is now very important to you that Communism should continue in Russia ; for have you considered, ladies and gentlemen, what your condition would be if Russia, with all its new resources, were forced back into imperialist capitalism ?

In my young days we were all mortally afraid of Russia. We talked about the Will of Peter the Great. Mr. Rudyard Kipling made his reputation as a patriotic laureate by denouncing the great White Bear, the power that meant to get its claws on India as a prelude to getting its claws on all Asia and dominating the whole world. I ask the mischievously foolish short-sighted gentlemen who write in the American newspapers denouncing Russia, telling every sort of silly lie about Russia, pretending that Russian Communism is bankrupt and the people starving, what they think they are doing ? Do they want the tsardom back again ? Tsar or no Tsar, do they want to start a Russian capitalist régime to compete with our own capitalists for our markets ? Do they want to dig up the White Bear from his Communist grave and resuscitate him with all his claws sharpened tenfold ?

What would be the effect if they succeeded ?

Suppose you sweep out Mr. Stalin as the monarchical Allies swept out Napoleon in 1815, and replace him by a dynastic Grand Duke and a government of old-fashioned diplomatists working with old-fashioned financiers, under the thumbs of old-fashioned capitalists fighting for new markets with the invincible Red Army created by Trotsky ! What will you have to do next ? You will have to quadruple your fleet. You will have to decuple your air force probably. You will not be able to sleep for dread of the White Bear.

Fortunately, Providence, having a kindly eye on America, has made Russia a Communist State ; and as long as it remains so you have nothing to fear from it. Your only anxiety ought to be as to what is going to happen in China ; and I sincerely hope for your sake that China will settle its scattered affairs by developing its present nucleus of Communism over its entire territory, so that China and Russia will be Communist powers. Then every American can sit under his vine and under his fig tree, and none shall make him afraid. If you cannot appreciate American Communism, at least learn to appreciate the benefit to America of having other countries Communistic. Think of the United States with not only Japan capitalist, but Russia capitalist and China capitalist ! You may well shudder.

Now let us return to the war debt. You want to get your money back. Well, the French owe you a lot of it. The French, following the example of most of the other States in Europe, tell you they are not going to pay : they will see you in Hades first. What is your remedy ? It is the familiar one of occupation and distraint. You can send over your United States Army to occupy France, and levy the sums due to you on the inhabitants. If France objects she can put fifteen million negro soldiers into the field against you without risking the life of a single Frenchman. Not much of a remedy that : is it ? You must make the best of the flat fact that France *can* pay you and wont. I daresay France will be nice enough to tip you perhaps a few million francs : the franc is worth four cents. You will have to accept it and look as pleasant about it as you can.

Now, England owes you more than France. But England does not refuse to pay. Like France she can pay ; and you know that she can. But you sometimes use a very thin argument. You say " If you English can afford to spend five hundred million dollars a year on an army and navy, you can afford to pay us what you owe us."

To that we reply " Come now, good old Stars and Stripes: you are spending six hundred million dollars a year on *your* army and navy. Can you blame us for doing the same ? You say to us ' Give up your soldiering ; and then we will see about letting you off your debt.' Suppose we say ' Give up your racketeering ; and then perhaps we will consider about paying. What is the use of paying you money to racketeer with ? ' " I wish I could tell you the figure which has been stated by one of your public men as the cost of racketeering in your country every year. I refrain because I came here firmly resolved that not a single word should pass my lips which could give the slightest offence to any American.

I might tell you that we in England are paying more than double the cost of our armaments every year in unearned incomes, even after deducting what we take back in taxation. But that is a delicate subject for both of us. The fundamental objection to making us pay is that we cannot do it with-

56

out pauperizing you. Remember our own predicament when we tried to make Germany pay. The Germans said " Well, you know that we have no gold in Germany to pay you with. What will you take instead ? "

We said " Pay in ships. Build ships. We need ships."

So they started paying in ships. Presently our Prime Minister found that all the ship-building yards on Tees and Tyne and Clyde had stopped work. The Germans had been given their job. The shipmasters and their workmen objected. The Prime Minister said " This must stop. You mustnt pay us in ships."

The Germans said " Well, what shall we pay you in ? Shall we pay you in steel ? "

The Prime Minister said " Yes : steel seems all right." But the British steel smelters said " No : it is not all right. You dont send any German steel in here to ruin us."

The Prime Minister then said to his staff " Will you kindly tell me what I am to ask these people to pay in ? It must be something that we do not produce ourselves." So his staff said " Potash." The Prime Minister accordingly said to the Germans " You must pay in potash."

Imagine a nation being called on to pay the cost of a European war in potash! Imagine the British Isles snowed under a mountain of potash! There was only one thing that could be taken from Germany without ruining some industry or another, and that was gold. So the Germans had to get gold in any way they could; and all the financiers said " Splendid! we will lend them the gold." That was a typical financier's solution : levy a colossal tribute on a defeated and penniless population, and prove their ability to pay by lending them the money to do it with! But what was the end of it? All the gold in the world poured through Germany into England and through England into the United States, which didnt need it. You, without knowing what you were doing, cornered the gold of the world, and broke the Bank of England. Nobody in Europe could get any more gold. You had it all here except what France held on to; and if you persuade France to pay up a little of her debt to you, she will only send you more gold. What use will it be to you? Ask your armies of the unemployed.

Is it not clear that to the extent that we are sending you all this gold, we are pauper-

izing you ? We are carrying you further on
the road towards making the entire country
an Atlantic City ringed round with a Miami
Beach. I seriously advise you to wipe the
slate and be content with having got rid of
the three empires and set up Communism
in Russia. It is very good value for your
money. Some of you may suspect me of
wanting to get a little off my income tax.
But I get a taxed income from the United
States as well as from England ; so what I
shall gain on the swings, I shall lose on the
roundabouts.

And now, what are you going to do about
it ? Do you not feel, as I turn these questions
inside out for you, that you need an Academy
of Political Science very badly ? And it must
be an American Academy and not a second-
hand European one. About fifty years ago
I and certain friends of mine—all of whom,
by the way, justified in after life their good
faith and their ability—established what is
called Fabian Socialism in England as a
political creed. It was from end to end
English. We knew all about Ferdinand Las-
salle and Karl Marx and the Social-Democrats.
We knew all about Fourier and Proudhon
and Blanqui in France. We knew about

59

Bakunin in Russia. But when we put our system before the English public there was not a single word about Karl Marx or any other foreign Socialist. From beginning to end Fabian Socialism was worked out on English lines with English thought, on English facts.

I strenuously advise you, when you come to back up this Academy of Political Science and to take your own part in its work of making a new Constitution, to make it an American Constitution from beginning to end. Dont bother about Karl Marx. Karl Marx was a mighty prophet; but almost all the administrative mistakes the Communists have made in Russia they have made for the sake of Marxist orthodoxy, whilst their success has been established under the leadership of Stalin, who is distinguished by the fact that he is a nationalist in Russia. Stalin says, in effect, " I will establish Communism in Russia and thereby set an example to Communists everywhere. If they do not choose to follow it, that is their lookout and not mine : Russia is large enough for me ; and I will work for the salvation of Russia and leave the other countries to save their own souls."

He is quite right. He has been successful along that line ; and I suggest to you that you in America should trust to that volcanic political instinct which I have divined in you and work out the whole thing for yourselves, from the American facts, with American thought, on American lines, until you finally turn the futile Hundredpercent American into a man who is not only one hundred per cent. an American but one hundred per cent. a statesman.

Now, ladies and gentlemen, there must be an end, even to speeches by Bernard Shaw. I have only to add that I am here to-night to pay back an old debt that I owe to America. In my youth I was in reaction against Fundamentalism, and combative for the advance of modern science and modern thought in the opposite direction. I was very full of evolution, of the new astronomical physics, and of the fine arts. But I knew nothing about the economic foundations of society, nor their importance in history and political science. Science was to me altogether outside politics. I did not know that there was such a thing as political science.

I went one night, quite casually, into a hall in London ; and there I heard a man deliver a speech which changed the whole current of my life. That man was an American, Henry George. He was from San Francisco. He had seen places like San Francisco grow up from mere camps into enormously rich cities; and he had noticed that the richer they became, the poorer they were. They had all got their politics into such a tangle, that American growth in riches, American advance in what we call civilization, was accompanied by an appalling reduction of the standard of life of the people. Everywhere Progress meant Poverty.

Well, Henry George set me on the economic trail, the trail of political science. Immediately afterwards I read Karl Marx and all the political economists of that time; but it was the American Henry George who made me do it; and therefore, as that was the beginning of my public life, I have thought it fitting that at the end of it I should come and repay to America a little of the impulse that Henry George gave me.

I have other debts to America. Some years afterwards, people even in England were in a great muddle as to the sort of person I was, because, not content with making one reputation, I had made about fifteen; and the people who knew one reputation didnt know the others ; so that Bernard Shaw seemed to be a dozen different persons. I remained incomprehensible until an American gentleman, the professor of mathematics to whom I have already alluded, Professor Archibald Henderson, presented me in a complete and intelligible shape to the public. The effect of that was very beneficial to me in England. I congratulated myself on having become one of the diversions of a mathematician. As a consequence, I got into mathematical shape and became a real person.

You now understand why, with almost every society in America asking me to speak, I chose out this particular body, the Academy of Political Science. It is the most important body in America to-day. The work that it is doing is the work that will save America if anything can save America. I shall not live to see that salvation ; but I hope I have prophesied it truly.